"_Living_" in the _Ditch_

1-Ditch **2**-Boys & **3,000**-Adventures

To - Andrei Jablokow
THANK YOU!
My life is much richer
through sharing our time
at Killer Keynote and
our speaker retreat.
You are a good man
with a kind heart.
— And A great sense of humor.
Thanks for your generous
spirit and changing the
lives of countless thousands.
Blessings Always to You.
Dave Wadsworth
1-19-19

1

"*Living*" in the *Ditch*
1-Ditch **2**-Boys & **3,000**-Adventures

Dedicated to:
Loretta M. Wadsworth

Written By
Dave **W. Wadsworth**

Editor in Chief:
Adam Lee **Wadsworth**

"*Living*" in the *Ditch*
1–Ditch, 2-Boys & 3,000-Adventures

Introduction

Two young boys living life full speed ahead. No cares, no time clocks, no regrets from yesterday, no concerns for tomorrow. Totally immersed in fun, fascination, fantasy & exploration. Enjoying God's indescribable creation in their own back yard. Curious and creative they lived for the moment in a playground of nature's delights. A playground that no amount of money could buy. Enjoy the exciting and special times these boys experienced for the meager price of their imaginations.

"_Living_" in the _Ditch_
1-Ditch, **2**-Boys & **3,000**-Adventures

Dedication:

This book is dedicated to my favorite author, Loretta Mae Wadsworth; aka "My Mom".

My mom was always reading, writing and taking pictures of birds and nature. I have to thank her for my early appreciation for, and knowledge of, birds and various kinds of wildlife. Mom has an inquisitive mind and a huge generous heart.

Thanks to mom I have always enjoyed an unquenchable thirst and deep passion for learning. Although reading was not my primary form of learning I always wanted to go, see, and do, new and exciting things.

In a strange mental growth spurt I have made amazing and almost unbelievable changes in my learning through reading.

Fact 1:

For 55 years of my life I read no more than a grand total of 25 books (I guess I preferred to watch the movie version). No, I'm not real proud of this under-achievement. I was well below the 1 book per year average of most adults. That dismal fact makes this next fact a point approaching unbelievable. Fact #2 is actually astonishing, fascinating and bewildering to myself and others.

Fact 2:

Since my lackluster reading start (25 books in 55 Years) I have documented reading over 1,000 books in under 2 years. (Insert GULP here)
WHAT? Yes, this sounds absurd to me as well. I know you are thinking my library must contain a mix of 20-minute quick read comics & coloring books. Yes, some books were fairly short. However, you should consider this ridiculous fact: These readings have included cover to cover of the Holy Bible 5 times in the last 12 months.

Yes, Genesis through Revelation. Wow, "What's up with that?", is a question I continue to ask myself.

My titles include **business, marketing, self - improvement, motivational, biographies, science, nature, sports stories, spiritual, history, humorous, sales, health & nutrition, technology, novels** and many more.

I came out of a dark period in mid-life that I describe as a valley that was deep, dark & soul crushing. It was like I was reborn and came alive like the first flowers of spring. I came alive with the vigor of a caged animal newly released into the wild. Since my reading speed is truly very average, I found that course of action tedious at best. Although I do read many print books I have found that Audible is my new best friend. It takes focused effort to average reading over one book per day.

As of this writing I'm finishing this calendar year (2018) with a books-read total just over 800. Technology has been a tremendous ally in my learning quest since the vast majority are audio books. Some books I like are not available on audio so I read them aloud into my phone voice recorder so I can listen to them over and over.

With all that said I want to credit my favorite author, my mom, with her constant encouragement and inspiration.

"*Living*" in the *Ditch*
1-Ditch, **2**-Boys & **3,000**-Adventures

I believe that:

Reading is **Learning**,

Learning is **Growing**,
growing leads to,

Happiness and **Success**.

Mom, thanks for helping me be happy and successful. I love you.

Dave W. Wadsworth   "Living" in the Ditch

"*Living*" in the *Ditch*

1-Ditch, **2**-Boys & **3,000**-Adventures

Doug, Mom and myself 2018

"_Living_" in the _Ditch_
1-Ditch, **2**-Boys & **3,000**-Adventures

Reflection & Action

Throughout this book I am going to ask you to do something very strange. You will have to buck all your school teachers, learned general rules of decent behavior and forge a new habit. At the end of each chapter I'm asking you to participate in an exercise that I know you will find challenging and rewarding. You will be asked a handful of questions regarding what you just read and then seriously consider your past, present and future responses. Yes, I am asking you to actually write in this book. Don't just think through these questions but actually write your thoughts on the pages provide. I promise you will be glad you did this. It's only a few minutes but they can be life altering minutes.

All the best to you.

"Living" in the *Ditch*

1-Ditch, 2-Boys & 3,000-Adventures

To contact the author: davewadsworth777@gmail.com
My Cell Phone # **is 812-499-5090**
Web site is: **Attitude.Coach**
My nature loving, tree eating website is: **ONEWAYTREES.COM**

ISBN- 9781791899981

Published by Dave W. Wadsworth Publishing
Printed in the United States of America
Edited by Adam Lee Wadsworth

"*Living*" in the *Ditch*
1-Ditch, **2**-Boys & **3,000**-Adventures

To my family—

On Holidays we meet at the home of one of my brothers. Christmas Eve is always at Kelly & Telesa's beautiful home in Odon, IN. All other holidays are at my brother Doug's house in Washington, IN. Doug, thanks for remodeling to accommodate our expanding family. Myra & her family have to fly in from San Diego.

These are always times of fun, food and fellowship. We make a large family circle and hold hands to pray and express thanks for all our blessings. I am always thankful for enjoying the best family in the whole world. Young and old and without exception the entire Wadsworth family rocks.

"*Living*" in the *Ditch*

1-Ditch, 2-Boys & 3,000-Adventures

Contents

1. Dam the Ditch..........................21

2. Creeping Crawdads...............53

3. Snakes Alive..............................68

4. Turtle Love..................................85

5. Minnows and Fish..............110

6. Little Blood Suckers............122

7. Cutting Your Feet Off.........131

8. Spiders of the Ditch (sorry, Book 2)

9. Fence #5 (Book 2)

10. Downstream Delights (Book 2)

11. Cows Floating Gifts (Book 2)

12. Strange Ditch Creatures (Book 2)

1. Dam the Ditch

In the distance, I could hear Doug, my little brother, yelling in a loud, rapid and panicked voice. Doug was a fairly quiet boy so just to hear him yelling was a very startling affair. I snapped to attention as I heard his cries;
"The Dam Broke!! The Dam Broke"!!

Immediately my ears perked up, my heart raced, my stomach leaped and my mind went into super speed. Instantly a million thoughts were bouncing around in my head like a giant box of ping pong balls thrown against a wall.

Again, Doug cried out;
"The Dam Broke!!, The Dam Broke"!!

This time I could tell he was running downstream as he screamed that frantic warning. My young mind was trying to process just exactly what those 3 little words meant.

THE.........DAM.........BROKE

Suddenly words like, Fear, Panic, Death, Devastation, Survival, Escape & Emergency flashed through my brain.

My shocked mind thought instantly; it's all over and I'm not ready for this life to end. I was in my happy place. I'm right where a boys' dreams of adventure come true. In a micro second I busted out "Please God, I'm just not ready".   And yet again the warning bell of those 3 little words rang out...... "The Dam Broke"!

Looking back, to that fateful day, I believe that was the first time I remember having a full blown panic attack. I don't really know if 5 & 6-year-old boys have heart attacks. What I do know, is that, in that instant, I was experiencing what felt like a total body, topsy-turvey, coming unhinged meltdown.

My brother Doug was just a year and a half younger than I and we were as tight as twins. I couldn't imagine my life without my little buddy. Like

Forrest Gump said about Jenny "we went together like peas and carrots".

Well, actually, let's rephrase that: From my earliest memories, eating peas has always made me gag. I think we went together like "Peanut Butter and Jelly".

Yep, PB & J. That All-American sandwich that is timeless and enjoyed by men, women and children alike.

Rabbit Trail to Guatemala, Central America.

Come to think of it, I believe that good ole peanut butter and jelly sandwiches actually saved my life once. A few years back our church youth group was on a weeklong mission trip to build a family home in Guatemala in Central America. After only a few days in Guatemala I remember getting a nasty stomach bug from eating the local food (could have been the water). I will kindly spare you the messy details of endless stomach cramps, diarrhea and vomiting. I was finally rescued by the great PB & J sandwich.

It was the only food that my body refrained from rapidly revolting in painful and disgusting ways.

On a more pleasant note concerning peanut butter and my childhood, I have to quickly share this. Mom and dad mixed up one of the tastiest sandwich concoctions of all time. It was smooth, creamy and irresistibly sweet. We would take a cereal bowl and mix in a blend of butter, peanut butter and maple syrup. Mixed all together and spread on bread it tasted heavenly.

Mixed together, Doug and I were so close it seemed we were nearly attached at the hip. I loved Doug and now realize, 50 years later, I wouldn't be half the person I am without his love, friendship and encouragement. I also realize millions of American children just don't have the blessing of enjoying such a rich and fulfilling relationship.

It was so much better than having a best friend in the neighborhood or just down the street. We shared bunk beds in our tiny bedroom. I really liked the bottom bunk and all the fun that came with it. I would often times hang a blanket down in front of my bunk and pretend it was my own little hideout, a secret cave or fortress. I felt safe and protected in that special fort of mine. My thoughts would sail away and magically explore exciting new wildlife adventures as I was nestled in my bunkbed castle. Countless nights I could hardly sleep just imagining what new creatures we would discover when the bright morning sun came back.

Doug was the youngest of 4 children God blessed to Joe and Loretta (Orender) Wadsworth. Kelly Joe was the oldest and he was 7 years ahead of me. Myra Jo was next and she was a feisty and beautiful girl just 3 years older. I think Myra had to be feisty to survive 3 brothers in our tiny 2-bedroom house. It is, what it is. No complaints, just struggles, blessings and fond memories. Given a second chance in life I would choose exactly my same home and family again.

A family chocked full of love, faith and solid moral character. The Wadsworth family (Robert Joe Wadsworth family) has produced generations of, (without exception) ethical individuals living lives of love, compassion, solid work ethic, generosity, honesty, pride, humility, etc., etc., etc. If it is a good, Godly or positive quality then the Joe Wadsworth family embraces it.

The small town of Plainville, Indiana (Population 500) was my home throughout my childhood. I always thought 500 was a nice round number. Funny thing how I thought we had a really small town until 30 years later I met Doug Sprague from Plainville, Illinois (Population 250). We were twice the size of Mr. Sprague's Plainville.

Like Andy Andrews, one of my favorite authors, says "I guess it is all in your perspective".

Speaking of Perspective; that reminds me ----

Do you know what the snail said as he rode on the back of the turtle?
............with raised arms the snail gasped to catch his breath and shouted:

wheeeeeeehhhh!!

Ah, Yes; the thrilling and "speedy" turtle ride of his life. PERSPECTIVE.

Turtle ride time is over so back "in the ditch".

I have always loved nature. I have always loved being outdoors and living totally immersed in it. Surrounded by the beautiful sights, interesting sounds, unique smells, the bitter/sweet tastes and the stimulating touches. My whole body and mind would come alive each and every minute that I "lived in the ditch". My senses were constantly abuzz and my ADD (Attention Deficit Disorder – or my failure to focus for more than a Texas second) was in full overdrive.

Doug and I were the richest kids in the whole world. No, not financially rich. However, each day, living in the ditch, we had it all. We didn't know any better.

It was the best feeling in the world. Kind of like the dog that takes a big drink out of the family toilet, licks his lips and exclaims, "man, it just doesn't get any better than this"!   Yuk! Nasty!

I have sometimes told people that we were so poor, we couldn't pay attention. However, we were never hungry, cold, naked or homeless. Well, sometimes we were hungry, cold and naked, but it was only by choice and that was not a lifestyle.

Dad and mom were fantastic parents made of the highest moral character. They both worked very hard to provide all the necessities of life, and then some. I often tell my mom still today that if I could start over again and choose any Dad and Mom in the world—Yes, I would choose Joe & Loretta Wadsworth.

My dad was a tall burley man just over 6 feet in height. He wore his hair in a crew cut (actually I think it was called a "Flat Top") like a proud soldier or sailor. On very rare occasions dad lost his temper and he was someone you wouldn't want to face off against. A large scary serious bull of a man came out. In those angry "bull" moments you just hoped you weren't wearing red that day. Red? Yes. The old story we were told is that an aggressive bull would charge the color red. So, don't cross a bull's pasture wearing red.

Actually, dad's anger events were about as brief in time as they were in occurrence. Joe Wadsworth was a firm man but extremely fair. He was friendly but very just. He was actually the kindest and biggest hearted person I've ever known (except maybe his mother—my grandma Floy (Sears) Wadsworth). A foul word rarely crossed his lips. His "never-met-a-stranger" friendly nature was engaging and inspiring. He created a glow of goodness that everyone, in his presence, both enjoyed and truly benefited from.

Rabbit trail for "PALS":

Dad modeled a tremendously positive attitude for his family & friends alike. I was blessed to inherit that "look for the good" attitude. In fact, my next book is entitled **"Attitude before Underwear"**. In that book I will be detailing the life-changing "Attitude" formula that I have developed.

I call my formula **PALS**.

PALS is actually an acronym for **P + A = LS.**

My speaking, coaching & training engagements involve implementing this formula into your Business, Organization or Family. Attitude is a critical success component every person should lock into their own minds.

P + A = LS stands for:

<u>P</u>roblems + <u>A</u>ttitude = <u>L</u>ife <u>S</u>uccess.

Since we all have Problems and all desire Life Success, the critical bridge involves something called our Attitude.

No matter what anyone says to you.
No matter what anyone does to you.
No matter the circumstances that surround you.

Our Attitude is the one thing that we have 100% control of. Our choice in our response to life. No matter how good or bad it seems, we ALWAYS have a choice of Attitude.

<u>The critical bridge to LIFE SUCCESS is your ATTITUDE</u>, pure and simple. Much more to come on this later.

Rabbit trail ends here so back to dad.

Although dad left high school early in his junior year (Odon, Indiana Bulldogs, Yeah! Rah!) he was a very smart man. He could study, investigate and solve countless problems, issues and complex situations. I remember the piles of mathematical problems dad would work through as he completed extensive mechanical and electrical engineering courses during his apprentice program at the Crane Indiana Naval Weapons Center.

In a nutshell – My dad (Robert Joseph Wadsworth) was AWESOME!!

Sorry for the rambling but I must get back in the ditch.

The ditch is formally and legally called Hannah Branch. Like a soaring eagle, its' flow was quiet, graceful and effort free. That relentless stream, like the rich red blood in my veins, flowed day after day throughout my childhood. Clear as crystal the ditch ran nearly year around. Only on rare occasions, during an extended summer dry spell, would the flow dry up. Those events occurred for just a brief few hours in the hot July afternoons.

The temporary dry ditch would leave only scattered deep pools for the minnows, fish and other water creatures to survive in. This ditch dry-up process was fairly rare. By some sort of magic, overnight, as Doug and I slept only 20 yards away, the ditch would come back to life and resume its' graceful flow.

The bottom, of the ditch, was lined with a golden brown sugar-like sand. This sand was carved into ripples and flowing tiny ridges only an inch or two high. These formations changed by the day, the hour, and sometimes minute by minute. Leaves, sticks, rocks, animals and various other forces would ebb and flow with the ditch currents to form and reform the wavy bottom. I remember sitting on the ditch bank, for what seemed like hours, watching the clear water shift, smooth, build and destroy fascinating and beautiful works of sand art. The tiny underwater sand ridges appeared like carefree snow drifts of brown sugar. Many of the peaks and ridges were followed by a thin line deposit of dark sand. This sand would often glisten with a magnificent purple color.

I also remember watching tiny pebbles, wood chunks and muscle shells bounce around behind these sand ridges. They were silently moved and propelled by invisible underwater currents. These objects danced like popcorn in the fancy movie theatre machines.

I have fond memories of being constantly mesmerized by the way the afternoon sun would sparkle and dance on the ripples of that clear flowing water. It was magical and I couldn't get enough of it. I think water of all kinds has that effect on people. From little children playing in mud puddles and ditches to adults drawn to lakes, ponds, rivers and oceans. It's a strange, magical and undeniable attraction.

Day after day, Doug and I would explore a different fascination and seek out a new adventure as we lived in the ditch. On this particular day we decided that we were going to play the role of human beavers. Great engineers of the wild. Designing and erecting an earthen dam was our adventure of the day. Our aim was to control & tame the mighty waters of Hannah Branch. We prided ourselves on great ingenuity and creativity.   We were the undisputed kings, when it came to mastering the all-powerful ditch and its wild creatures living there.

Together our minds were constantly discovering ways to hunt down and capture the vast array of minnows and fish. Fish were always schooling in the depths, hiding under the floating moss strands or frantically darting from shore to shore. The fish, like white-tailed deer, were instinctively skiddish and behaving nervously. Doug and I enjoyed constantly learning new techniques to capture them.

The emerald green moss strands were very fascinating to me. They were long and flowing like strands of beautiful green hair. Some strands would grow several feet long and become as thick as huge rope. Fish and minnows would swim and hide just below these strands. The green flowing strand provided a perfect visual barrier from themselves and aggressive predators. Many creatures were always wanting to catch and eat them. Doug & I were not looking to cook and eat the fish but we were relentless on the hunting & catching part.

Sometimes Doug and I would run our wire screen nets under the strands and capture an amazing variety of fish, crawdads and water-bugs. We would scoop up the entire section of moss and then lift it out of the water in our metal net. On the bank we would then dig through massive amounts of moss to find a bonanza of marine life. It was like combing and picking through a mass of wet hair to find hidden creatures. That was like a treasure hunt and oh what fun it was to experience.

Rabbit trail to Central America:

A brief story about combing and picking through hair. Several years back our church youth group went on a mission trip to Honduras in Central America. We mainly helped to remodel an Orphan School for handicapped and orphaned elementary aged children.

The school was actually founded and run by a retired lady from Spencer, Indiana. She was a retired "Stone Cutter" who had done work on the Monument Circle statues in downtown Indianapolis. This lady used her retirement funds to buy, refurbish, and run this school. It's all pretty amazing that she was living just 25 miles from my Indiana hometown. Now as adults, we meet in Central America because of our love for children.

While in Honduras, we had a church service with the local community. I was sitting behind a couple of beautiful young girls approximately 10 years old when the "event" happened. I noticed that a small bug appeared in one of the girls' gorgeous black flowing hair. I instinctively reached out to pluck and chuck the little bug. As I reached, a strange sense of; whoa Dave, you don't know this girl and we are not in America, stopped me in mid reach. I slowly pulled my bug plucking hand back and quietly watched with awkward silence. To my horror and disgust her hair suddenly came alive with a dozen such bugs. They would come to the surface and then quickly crawl back into her thick black hair and disappear. That was more than a little creepy. I think my skin literally crawled for a week as I tried to shed that image from my mind. Obviously the image is still pretty clear some 15 years later. Buurrrrr...Yukkk.

Sorry, back in the ditch we go.

For Doug and myself, one of our greatest ideas of adventure and conquest involved a masterful plan to "Dam the Ditch". Most of the ditch ran only about 6 or 8 inches deep. Various pools would sometimes reach depths of 20 inches at their deepest place. On occasion a shallow sandbar fully exposed the rich golden bottom in small areas. These sandbars stood only an inch or two above the flowing water. Here is where we could often times find a turtle or snake warming themselves in the hot afternoon sunshine.

We would first select the perfect dam site and then design our masterpiece.   This ideal dam site would be chosen based on many engineering factors that I will detail later. We took great pride in our ingenuity and resourcefulness.

Once this engineering feat "the dam" was completed we would watch in delight as the downstream water quietly disappeared. Methodically and magically our fishing trap would appear. With the dam in place the receding water would automatically leave the minnows and fish in the scattered remaining pools with nowhere to hide or escape to. A few unlucky stragglers were actually caught and lay freaked-out, flopping and completely helpless on the strange new dry creek bed.

I truly can't remember exactly how or when we discovered the "Dam-Fishing" technique. It was literally, shall we say, like "shooting fish in a barrel". Only the barrels were little pools made by our damming up the ditch. The remaining pools reduced the water area of the ditch to about 5% of its' original size. This would give us a much greater advantage in capturing our stranded little aquatic prey. It worked every time and we always caught a bounty of fish, crawdads & minnows.

The dam site would be selected based on the depth of water, width of the ditch, and best available building materials nearby. The ditch bottom was like brown sugar sand and so it was very limiting in its use for a very large dam. It would easily melt away as water flowed over and through it. We would often times dig deep with our bare hands to the cool clay-like mud under the sandy bottom. We also found a great dirt supply along the banks of the ditch.

For our larger dams we often times added in sticks, bricks and leaves for reinforcing materials. Since dad seeded grass and mowed our home side of the ditch bank we were forbidden from excavating extra dirt from there. Our home was a mere 50 feet away and dad would have skinned us boys alive (ok, maybe just a hard spanking) if we damaged our side of the ditch.

However, as luck would have it, the other bank was wild and wooly with plants, animals and creatures of all kinds. That wild bank was bordered by a farmer's corn field so digging much needed clay-like dirt from there was a bonanza for us. Many times we would find a concrete block or a brick bat (Grandma Hazel Orender's word for a brick) we could strategically place for additional dam height and stability.

Rabbit Trail for Abe Lincoln.

My grandma was Hazel Ayers who married my Grandpa (moms' dad) who was Ivan Orender. The Orender family has its' roots back in a small Kentucky town called Hodgenville. This is the birthplace of President Abraham Lincoln. So, it is conceivable that my great, great, great, great....Grandpa lived near and played with Abe Lincoln as a boy. Interesting isn't it?

In addition to that, I currently live in Boonville, Indiana where it is said that "Lincoln learned the Law". In fact, we are a mere 15 miles from where Lincoln was raised as a young man. The area near Gentryville, is the home of Lincoln State Park and the Lincoln National Boyhood Memorial.

Ok, back in the Ditch.

The ditch was typically 4 to 6 feet wide from bank to bank. Our selected construction site would have water only about 6 inches deep.   The perfect size for two industrious, adventure seeking, nature loving little boys. We would erect the dam about 75% of the way across the ditch and allow water to flow around the open end. We would then stockpile many handfuls of mud to make the final span of the dam. In a mud piling frenzy, Doug and I would quickly & completely cut off the ditch flow. At this point we had a few minutes to step back and admire our engineering masterpiece and pat ourselves on the back for being "masters of the ditch".

The newly erected dam was always a beautiful and rewarding site to behold but it gave us only minutes to work with. We quickly began exploring the pools of trapped fish and selecting our prime targets downstream. Usually we would go downstream together and see what rich treasures the dry ditch bed revealed. Oh, how exciting those first moments were. Two barefoot boys treasure hunting in the ditch was an amazing rush of excitement. Our minds told us "it just doesn't get any better than this"!

Rabbit trail for Editors reflection:

Remember me talking about how refreshed the dog was after drinking from the family toilet? Ok, well, it gets a little gross here so you may want to hold your nose, ears and eyes. (YOU TOO MOM)

Picture this: The summer days are hot. The little boys get thirsty. The ditch water looks clear & clean.

Yes, indeed we would, on occasion, cup our hands and take a nice long drink of the refreshing, cool ditch water. Slurp, Slurp.

Only natural, right? No harm in that?

NASTY #1   Well, I haven't described how...on occasion, we would have to go poty #1. No time to run in the house to do it properly, right? Yep, Pee Pee right in the ditch. YUK!

It gets worse.

NASTY #2 - Our rural sanitation situation included a pipe with our "gray water" (the liquid from our home flushings & washings) emptied into that "pure" clean drinking water. DOUBLE YUK!!

Oh, Yes – it gets worse.

NASTY #3 - I didn't tell you that Farmer Smith just 100 yards up the ditch watered his many cows in the ditch. Ok you say. A little cow slobber won't hurt. Right, but the regular flow of #2 Brown Floaters (cow pooh) we constantly watched float by would make the average adult gag. TRIPLE YUK!!!

Back to the "Dam-Fishing"

After selecting our best fishing targets, we would quickly spring into action. We used many methods to catch the minnows and fish but our favorite was the use of a 2-foot square scrap piece of flexible screen door wire mesh. We could easily bow the mesh like a half pipe and tilt the front end down while raising the back end. We would then slide the wire mesh along the bottom and through the water to scoop up the darting minnows. When we lifted the screen out of the water we immediately knew we were super star fishermen. Our hearts pounded with pride when a dozen or more minnows and little fish would remain flopping helplessly on the small screen.

Victory-Victory-Victory!!!

Now what? What do you do with such a bountiful harvest of minnows and fish? Again, learning from previous experiences, we strategically placed a variety of glass jars and plastic containers, filled with ditch water, along the ditch bank. These containers were perfect to put the newly captured live fish in. Usually mason jars, gallon sized old glass root beer jars and empty coffee cans would do the trick. We had to work quickly with not a second to spare. This fishing party was short lived because as the downstream went dry the upstream got deeper by the minute. We were battling nature on several fronts at once and we loved every action filled second of it.

Quickly, Doug or I would have to run back upstream to check the dam site and access the situation. We would normally have to pile much more mud on top of the dam to keep the rising water at bay. We would usually be so excited about catching the trapped fish that we would wait too long to go back and check on the dam. This delay could be disastrous.

Usually there would be one or two small overflow areas that needed immediate patching before we could return to our fish catching frenzy. This special day we kept adding to the top of the dam and it was by far the largest we had ever dreamed up or constructed. It was a huge mega-dam (At least for two young boys).

On this particular day the fish catching was tremendous and our hearts nearly pounded out of our chests. We soon found a shallow fish pool absolutely loaded with minnows. They were flopping and flipping by the hundreds. It was fantastic to see. Then came the shock of our lives. You can imagine our horror as we approached to see a very large brown and tan striped water snake in the middle of this shallow pool.

He was a monster at 5 feet in length. Stretched out he was longer than we were tall. Yikes! He was gobbling up the helpless flopping minnows at lightning speed. It was an awesome sight to behold and clearly frightened Doug and I half to death.

I honestly remember nearly wetting my pants when we were first startled by the snake. He would pull his head back like stretching back a rubber band and then he would strike. Then he would coil back and strike again, and again. He was gobbling down minnows like the Indiana State Fair hotdog eating champion.

WOW, this was a site to see. We ended up trying to get forked sticks to safely catch the snake but couldn't seem to find any large enough. This was a beast of a snake at least 2 feet longer than we were tall. We started yelling and making lots of noise and finally managed to scare off the snake.

That beast of a snake had a feast of savagery in that minnow pool. I think the "attack" actually lasted for several minutes. It was a brutal and savage act for two scared little boys to watch. Again, I must say that I can honestly remember thinking I was so scared I nearly wet my pants.

Doug and I then continued searching downstream from pool to pool for treasures of trapped minnows and water creatures. We were so distracted by the snake and abundance of fish that we soon lost track of time. I got a nervous flutter in my stomach as I realized our very large dam could be in jeopardy. With this jolt, of fear, I quickly ordered Doug to run up the dry ditch bed to check on the dam. Seconds after Doug left I turned my attention to bigger and better fish pools some distance downstream.

I immediately became engrossed in the excitement of the hunt. My mind was focused on fish and nothing else. It's funny how some things never change. My mind can change directions in a micro-second and then change again at full speed. It's like the image from our cartoon days. The "Road Runner" and "Coyote" have nothing on me and my crazy brain.

Then disaster struck hard. My dream adventure was abruptly halted in one brief moment. With a loud screech, squeal and smash it all came crashing down. I was so excited and determined to catch more fish that it took several warning screams to get my attention.

The Dam Broke! The Dam Broke! The Dam Broke! Doug was running and yelling at the top of his lungs. It caught me off guard and I was instantly shocked into a state of Fear and Uncertainty. I soon calculated I only had a few minutes, no, maybe only seconds now. Suddenly, a torrent of flood waters came crashing down to where I was.

Again, I remember a fright that nearly made me wet my pants. Wow, I was not ready for all this. It changed everything. As the waters raced down the dry ditch bed the remaining pools were instantly engulfed and disappeared. This swift flood freed the trapped fish and minnows to again swim and escape danger as they had only hours before. Up and down the beautiful ditch they could now swim and dart and play. Doug and I, on the other hand, found ourselves once again beaten back by the simple constant flow of nature. Always so beautiful and yet so relentless and powerful. Such is life that special day for Doug and I "Living in the Ditch".

End of Chapter One.

"**Living**" in the **Ditch**
1-Ditch, **2**-Boys & **3,000**-Adventures

Dam the Ditch Reflection and Action

WOW, that was a long chapter. Sorry. My Bad.

Action 1.   **Write** briefly about a childhood memory that included nature and your creative interaction with it.

Action 2. Plan and do something this week that will bring back that same sense of joy and adventure you shared in Action 1.

Action 3. **Plan** an activity you can **do each week** to take you back to that amazing child-like carefree world. Be sure it is not Illegal, Immoral or Fattening. (Insert Smile)

2. Creeping Crawdads

Ouch!, Ouch!, Ouch!

Doug jumped up yelling and shaking his hand and arm. He leaped and pranced around in a funny dance. Finally, the "Granddaddy" released its sharp large front pinching claw from Doug's finger. That little pinching monster, now free, and Doug glad to see him go, crawled quickly back into the safety of the ditch. Those pinching boogers draw blood sometimes. Every single time they got the chance to pinch you it sure did hurt.

Crawdads we called them. Other people call them Crayfish. Either way, the ones we called Granddaddys can sure pinch the snot out of you any place they find bare skin. Actually, with those huge front claws they can inflict their painful torture even through your clothes.   They look like miniature lobsters and sure can defend themselves when they are cornered. Cornering and catching crawdads, is exactly what Doug and I did, almost daily, as we "Lived" in the Ditch.

Living in the Ditch does seem like an exaggeration for the life and times of two little boys. Truth be told, I can honestly remember many times hearing that phrase spoken. I still remember the funny tone of voice used when mom or dad would talk to folks around Plainville. While talking about their young boys Dave and Doug, they would repeatedly use the phrase "Those boys practically Live in the Ditch".

I'm sure it would have taken the Town Marshall, State Police and the Indiana National Guard to keep us out of that ditch. Two little adventurous boys on a mission can scheme and scam their way into all kinds of trouble. Since dad worked all the time, and mom worked off and on, it was impossible for them to keep us out. I'm so glad they didn't try too hard. It's a minor miracle we didn't die of tetanus or get lockjaw or any of those other things we were constantly lectured on. I can honestly say that a million dollars' worth of toys couldn't replace the life Doug and I enjoyed in that ditch.

Have you ever seen a simple mud puddle that a child could resist? Water and kids are metal and magnets. Ditches, puddles, ponds and any body of water are undeniably irresistible for kids. I think it is especially attractive for little boys.

Sometimes I wish as an adult I would lighten up and splash around in some mud puddles from time to time. I heard Robin Sharma, another author I like a lot, describe adults as deteriorated kids. You never hear kids say, "I just can't forgive so and so for what they did last year" or "My past is just so awful that I can't get over it". No sir, a kid's mindset of light hearted faith, love, fun and forgiveness seems to get squashed out of them way too early in life. We should live, especially in our relationships, more like **children** AND **dogs.**

Doggie Diversion:

That makes me think;

Question?

Do dogs have heart attacks?

Are they ever stressed, depressed and have high blood pressure or strokes?

My dog Sadie seems to be happy and free spirited in every part of life. She just wants to smile, wag her tail and spread sunshine and cheer all over the house. What an awesome attitude. I petted my neighbor's dog yesterday and he said she never met a stranger. Wow, just like my dad. I liked her immediately.

Back in the ditch with those crawling pinching machines.

Crawdads are strange and fascinating creatures that seem to be everywhere. They love water and even wet areas in your yard where there is no standing water. You have seen their work and might not have realized it. A majestic 6-inch-tall castle built of small marble-like balls of mud. I remember sitting along the grassy ditch bank being very quiet and really still (a feat of magnificence for a 6-year-old boy) as I waited for the crawdad to emerge. He would climb from his tunnel and continue building his little castle. It took amazing patience to set there long enough for the crawdad to feel safe enough to come out and roll more mud marbles. It was so fascinating to watch him roll and shape and place each small mud marble. That was a rare treat of fun.

Spider Sidebar here:

You want to really be amazed check this out. On a quiet evening as the sun fades away and darkness sets in, just sit and watch a spider magically and purposefully weave its web. A magnificent engineering masterpiece to snare nearby flying insects. It is pure poetry in motion. Speed, agility, accuracy, explodes into an engineering marvel in mere moments. The beauty and grace are a stunning thrill to behold. I often observe this magnificent event just inches away from my kitchen sink through the crystal clear window pane. I will tell you much more about spiders in the following chapters.

In the ditch we loved to hunt down the crawdads. We would plan our unique ambush and boldly snatch them. Our curiosity was always piqued by their odd monster-like features. Sometimes we would hold them up and try to figure out all the moving parts. Those dark bulging beady eyes. The super long hair-like whiskers sticking out in front. The two huge sharp and prickly front claws. The numerous pairs of baby claws running the length of its body. The scaled and sectioned folding tail. The fanned out scaly end of the tail. Wow, what a creature to behold. We would play with them for several minutes and then usually free them to crawl right back into the ditch.

The ones we called "Granddaddys" were the big aggressive ones with the large sharp front pincher claws. I remember all their legs had tiny claws which looked really funny. The front claws were huge, sharp and powerful. Sometimes we would find just the large pinchers lying along the ditch bank and imagine how huge that one must have been. Apparently the raccoons and other animals liked eating the crawdads they would catch at night.

Those large claws were a colorful combination of red, orange, green and white. They were made of very hard bone-like material and were strangely smooth and harshly pitted at the same time. The two pincher points that came together were like a very sharp, extra tooth that was uniquely fitted on the end of each claw. Almost like some type of inter-changeable specialty tip.

One day we had caught two or three large crawdads and decided to play gladiator games with them. We made a tiny circular arena from sticks and small rocks we found around our driveway. Several large Silver Maple trees lined our ditch bank and were constantly dropping dead limbs & twigs into our yard.

Our finished "gladiator" arena was about 20 inches in diameter. When fully constructed the stick sides were probably 2 or 3 inches tall. We had high hopes that this arena would serve as a great battleground. We anticipated that it would add hours of fun and entertainment.

We placed the crawdads inside the arena thinking they would wrestle and fight. Since we didn't want to get pinched we would each use a short guide-stick. Like puppet strings, the guide-stick would move, push and guide the gladiators. Before long we realized that all they wanted to do was crawl under the sticks to escape. They wanted to find the fastest way back into the ditch. I think they were much smarter than we were. You could tell they instantly knew this was a stupid and pointless endeavor. With their disinterest we soon lost our interest and so that was a very short lived silly event.

I never remember killing any crawdads. Actually I don't recall killing hardly any of the ditch creatures. The exception to that, of course, was blood sucking critters likes ticks, leaches and mosquitos. They all got the death penalty. Execution was swift and sure when we go ahold of those nasty parasites. Stay tuned and I'll tell you all about those little suckers later on.

One thing we did figure out about crawdads was that they have to come up for air and can't stay under water forever like a fish. We would pour water down their castle topped holes. We found these mini-castles all along the ditch bank. The hole-filling method would usually flush them out. They would need air and would eventually crawl out where we could catch them. We used our moms mason canning jars for this feat and just kept dipping into the ditch for refills until they had to come out. We had to keep the holes filled up to the top in order for this operation to work. If the crawdad wasn't in the hole or he was stubborn and took too long, we would give up the quest and move on to other adventures.

Catching crawdads was tons of fun and sometimes not that easy. Doug and I often used the 2-foot square screen door mesh with great effectiveness. Crawdads are funny to watch when they are under water. When they feel threatened they flip their tail and it sends them rocketing backwards. It was so cool to watch them do this. Even the tiny crawdads used this flip and zoom maneuver. The little ones were fun to watch since their flip and zip wasn't as effective. We could easily snatch these little ones up after they would travel only about 6 inches.

Momma crawdads were pretty amazing creatures that we would catch from time to time. If you look closely at crawdads they have dark beady little eyes like black BBs. They also have long cat-like whiskers coming out of their face. Speaking about the face, I must be blunt here --- "the crawdad has one seriously ugly mug". We used to say it was a face only a mother could love.

We guessed that what we caught were momma crawdads because they would have a huge cluster of black eggs bunched up under their tails. It was fascinating to study this amazing site. We never played with the momma crawdads but quickly put them back into the ditch. Their tail was full of dark colored eggs that looked like a cluster of 100 or more crawdad eyeballs. Pretty weird. At least Doug and I thought so.

One day Doug caught a large crawdad and it had a really soft shell. We never understood why this occurred but over time we caught many that had the soft shell. I think it was some kind of genetic defect that left them weak and vulnerable. Usually the shells were firm and made a solid place to squeeze and pick them up.

WARNING!!! If you are going to catch crawdads, with your bare hands, you need to have a safe technique. Doug and I were proud of our superior intellect when it came to mastering the monsters of our ditch. Along with the wire-mesh fishing method I remember a clever technique we used for handling crawdads. We would put one hand out in front of the big crawdads as a distraction. At the same time, we slyly slipped our other hand in behind them for the capture.

These beasts would always rear up those large front claws in a defensive move to guard against the impending attack. When they raised up those big sharp claws, that's when the real action happened. In a move of stealth and unnoticed trickery, I would then slip my other hand in behind the claws and their beady eyes.

With my thumb on one side and index finger on the other I could safely make the catch. You had to be fairly quick and decisive or the little snapper would turn and give you an especially nasty pinch. When you closed your thumb and index finger in against their shell you had to get a good hold so the rascal didn't wriggle free. You also didn't want to squeeze too hard and crack the shell and hurt the crawdad. Hurting the ditch creatures always upset me and seemed mean and pointless. Like I said before, only the diseased, nasty blood sucking parasites suffered our wrath.

The behind-the-head method was much like what we used in catching and handling snakes. The snakes, especially the big 4 or 5-foot-long monsters, made me pretty nervous to handle. I bet if mom watched us handle those big guys she would have fainted. Some of these snakes were much longer than we were tall. We had to be really careful to get a firm neck hold. If the snake ever slipped your grip there was surely a painful bite coming your way.

Wow, were we two young beast-masters or what?

It was great fun "Living" in the Ditch.

"Living" in the *Ditch*
1-Ditch, **2**-Boys & **3,000**-Adventures

Creeping Crawdads -- Reflection and Action

WOW, I hope that chapter brought back a few memories.

Action 1. **Write** briefly about a childhood memory that included live crawdads and your interaction with them.

Action 2. Look for a ditch or wet area where crawdads hang out near where you live. **Plan and go** there this week. Stop and check out those mud marble castles.

Action 3. **Plan** an activity you can **do each week** to take you back to that amazing child-like carefree world. Be sure it is not Illegal, Immoral or Fattening. (Insert Smile)

3. Snakes Alive

**Strike, gulp, gobble, recoil, repeat.
Strike, gulp, gobble, recoil, repeat.**

Again and again and again. It was savage. It was brutal. It was breathtaking. And yes, it was pants-wetting scary for two barefoot young boys just a few feet away. The huge brown and tan stripped monster snake was devouring helpless minnows and small fish faster than you could yell – Mommy! – Help! – Stop! – Oh No!

The large mud, sand, and stick dam Doug and I masterfully designed and built was just a dozen yards upstream. The dam drained the once lively flowing ditch in just a few minutes. Left behind were scattered pools of shallow water absolutely teaming with aquatic creatures. They were bunched in like a can of live wiggling sardines. With no hope of escape the minnows, crawdads and various water bugs didn't have a clue.   They must have been asking themselves how or why their watery paradise just shrank into puddles of overcrowded prisons.

The creatures were clueless, to the fact, that they were pawns in a master plan designed to quickly enslave them. The small puddles stopped the easy and countless escape options available by the full flowing ditch. Minnows would dart forward, backward and side to side in a series of maneuvers to evade capture.

Moss, algae, weeds, sticks and rocks created an abundance of cover and protection while the ditch flowed full. With a rapidly draining ditch those safety options were all removed and rendered useless. It was now a prison of merely a dozen small puddles.

Back to the "Attack"

Doug and I were not prepared for the savage and startling sight that warm summer day. Expecting a bonanza of easy fishing we were more than a little surprised when we came around the corner. In that instant we came face to face with this massive beast devouring our newly snared prisoners.

We knew this huge aggressive snake had no clue why he just hit the jackpot of free and easy fish.   He also wasn't about to look a gift horse in the mouth. (Hey kids and city slickers, you may want to google that one). That beast was going for broke and looked like the grand prize hot dog eater at the state fair. It was one of those rare strange sights that when it's all over you just shake your head and say "WOW, I ain't never seen nothin' like that before" "That was Awesome!".

Rabbit Trail for Chris Farley:

Chris Farley was a very talented and super funny actor from his work on "Saturday Night Live". He also acted in numerous movies including "Tommy Boy" (one of my favorites). His early death was a huge loss to so many. I actually have a dear friend from Atlanta, Dan Adkins, who worked with Chris Farley and dozens of famous actors in movies and Saturday Night Live. In fact, you may remember the Saturday Night Live skit with Patrick Swayze & Chris Farley doing their famous Chip-n-Dales mock dance. My friend Dan was on that crew just a few feet out of sight from that skit. Dan has some awesome stories and really enjoyed working with all the stars, except one.

Anyway, in the movie "Tommy Boy" Chris and his fellow actor Dana Carvey hit a large buck deer while traveling across the country on a sales trip. Not sure what to do with the "dead" deer, they placed it in the back seat of the car.

Just to let you know, at the beginning of the trip the car was a beautifully restored classic convertible. Quickly, the two rushed on down the road to their next sales call. The large back-seat deer suddenly came back to life. Shocked by the deer "awakening" they slammed on the brakes bringing the car to a screeching halt. The two men jumped out of the car in total disbelief. They then witnessed that huge buck deer rip that convertible to shreds. It then stepped onto the car hood and then calmly bounded off into the woods.

The two men were obviously stunned at the entire episode they just witnessed. After a moment of awkward silence, Chris Farley said with great enthusiasm,

"That......Was....... AWESOME!!"

So now, if you remember that part of the movie, that is the exact feeling Doug and I had. We were watching that massive snake with all its' vicious fervor "Strike, Gobble, Recoil.... Repeat". It was attacking and eating those defenseless fish like a starving savage.

That sneaky snake encounter, though our most frightening by far, was just one of many run-ins we had with those slithering creepers in our ditch.

In life, small boys like us trusted and believed just about everything our wise old father told us concerning nature and life in general. This was "exception to-the-rule" time. Dad told us not to be afraid of the snakes we would find in and around our ditch. He would say, "because they are more afraid of you than you are of them".

NOT! NOT! NOT!

Ha! Ha! very funny dad.

Since we didn't speak slithering snake tongue we couldn't ask them if this was true. But, I don't think any of those creepy snakes ever "wet their pants" when they saw us boys for the first time. It was a fact that first sightings of any snake by bare foot little boys causes a real fear jolt to the heart.

Rabbit Trail for Toad Frog Pee:

Here is the animal exception to that "wet-your-pants" rule. Each summer our yard would come alive with what we called Toad Frogs. These toads were cute but not cuddly. They were slow and easy to catch as they hopped through the grass.

The tan bodies were loaded with light tan and brown bumps and warts. I'm not sure how it happened but one day I learned that if you ever licked your fingers after handling a toad frog you got an instant nasty bitter taste. I think we played with these critters nearly every day. We did learn the nasty lesson that every time we picked up a toad frog we were guaranteed a good pee on the hand. Sometimes we also got the full flood that ran down our arm too.

Usually it was startling and I'm guessing that was the idea. The toad pee would normally cause a quick reaction and we dropped them back in the grass. Stay tuned because Toads & Frogs are coming later.

Snakes: We did observe some very colorful, graceful, and beautiful snakes though. Like the Blue Racer that sprinted into the corn field one sunny afternoon. He was for sure the most brilliantly colored and definitely the fasted snake of all. The Blue Racer was only spotted high on the bank and never in the water.

One day I recall our encounter with a very, very long black snake. This Black Snake was so fat and long that we thought at first it was just a part of a black garden hose. Woops, that hose is alive (insert boys wet your pants here) and we decided to run away super-fast. I remember being so scared that it was hours later before we dared to come back near where we spotted that lively wriggling black hose.

Rabbit Trail for Road Kill:

Speaking of big snakes, I remember as a little boy we would go visit my cousin Lee who lived out in the woods near Farlan. One day we (several young boys) were riding in the back of my cousin Leroy's pickup truck through the country side. Riding in the back of an open pickup truck bed was pretty common back then and I remember lots of such trips.

That particular day we weren't moving fast but all the sudden Leroy stopped the truck, jumped out of the driver's seat, and grabbed a huge black snake in the road. Lee, myself and my brother scrambled from the bed of the truck just in time to see cousin Leroy pick up this super long snake by the tail. He held it up for just a few moments while it wiggled and lunged trying to bite him. Then I saw Leroy sling the snake forward like a rope and then with a sudden jerk he yanked it back like cracking a leather whip. The violent whipping action exploded that huge snakes head in an instant.

Wow, that was creepy, powerful, and frightening all at the same time. What do you say to something like that? My brother Doug, Lee and I just stood there numb. We were trying to process all this craziness that had erupted and ended in less than a few minutes. Cousin Leroy just calmly hurled the lifeless creature into the road ditch without a word. I was thinking, I sure hope I don't make cousin Leroy mad at me or he might take a notion to snap my little neck like that.

OK, back in our ditch we wade on.

Doug and I were always amazed at how fast the water snakes could swim. Usually they would wind their way across the top of the water. They swam as smooth as milk weed silks floating on the summer breeze.

It was fascinating to see them slither through the water as graceful as a twirling ballerina. They would have their head up and wind from side to side in a steady rhythm. When they would catch a glimpse of us they immediately darted under water and right to the mossy bank.

It seemed like a snake could dart away and escape our capture faster than a bunny rabbit. Once they reached the tall weeds and grass they were home safe.

The little Garter Snakes, we constantly found in our yard, were about as cute and unintimidating as a snake can be. When dad was hoeing weeds in the garden or mom would scream, as a snake invaded the yard, he would act swiftly and separate the head and body of that unlucky beast with a single strike. After the brutal event dad would toss the carcass into the ditch for the coons to eat as they made their nightly patrol. I think dad thought the dead snake body would serve as a stern warning for other snakes to stay out of the yard.

Snake Guts Galore: We had a frightening encounter with a very large brown and tan water snake in our yard one day. That snake was very aggressive and dad quickly got the hoe and chopped this one into pieces. It was near the house and mom was scared to death of it.

After dad had rescued mom, then her boys we were allowed to check out this lifeless creature. As we examined the snake it appeared to have a very large lump in its body. Dad thought maybe it had eaten a large mouse so we cut it open to investigate. Wow, to our amazement it was full of slimy little baby snakes about the size of very large fishing worms.   They looked a lot like night crawlers. From the looks of these little snakes it wasn't going to be long before our yard would have been full of these little creepers.

Catching Snakes: By far the majority of snake encounters ended peacefully. Doug and I would often times catch the snakes and play with them just a little while and then release them back into the ditch. Sometimes, to prove our wild animal mastery, we would carry them over and show them to mom or grandma before we let them go.

Dave W. Wadsworth   "Living" in the Ditch

We learned a tremendous amount about animals from Dad and watching Wild Kingdom on TV. I'm not sure exactly how we developed our snake catching technique but it proved quite effective. Once we cornered a snake we would get a long stick with a forked branch at the end.

We usually would snap off the end fairly short to make it work right. We held the snake down with another stick and then used the forked one to hold the snake just behind its head. When we had a firm hold on the snakes head we would reach behind, just like the crawdads, and hold with our thumb and index finger just behind the head. We made sure to have a firm grip before removing the forked stick.

When you picked up the snake it would immediately wrap its whole body around your arm. If you didn't get the grip right the snake would pull its head away hard and give you a nasty bite. Since we never got bit we must have done it right. I wish I could boast like that about the crawdads. Ouch, Ouch, Ouch was my reaction after many painful pinches from those rascals.

Many times we grabbed the tail and the head so the snake couldn't do the arm wrap. After a few minutes you could feel the snake relax as it no longer seemed threatened by our holding it. Like I said, we mostly caught, briefly played with, and then released the snakes.

Weird Story: Super tiny Thread Snakes were actually strange snake-like creatures we would often find in the ditch. They surely weren't true snakes since they were a mere 3 inches long and as thin as a course brown strand of moms mending thread.

These thread snakes were very interesting to watch. Dark brown in color, we would watch them swim through the water in the exact same wriggling motion of the true and large snakes. I remember catching them and while in my hand they would make a striking action as if to bite me.

Of course they were so very tiny that they would slightly stick to my finger but much too small to penetrate my skin.   With miniature fangs it was a funny and futile act. It would be like me trying to bite an elephant on the leg. (Picture that one in your mind)

They were so tiny we couldn't even see a mouth not to mention fierce fangs or sharp teeth. They sure would wiggle around in your hand. It was like a magical piece of thread coming to life and dancing about.   What a strange and fascinating creature to observe and play with.

Looking back, I don't know why we didn't get a magnifying glass to get a much better view of these weird critters. It was probably a combination of: 1. My very short attention span and, 2. Being surrounded by so many other fascinating critters to play with.

Kind of like two little boys sitting paralyzed in a room full of toys. Too many choices and too little time.

Good news – lots of toys to play with.
Bad new – overwhelmed with too many options for fun.

I think as adults we often get paralyzed in the same way. Too many good or ok options for spending our time. We need to just take a few minutes and quietly set down on the ditch bank of life. In that quiet-time, we should focus on the few truly valuable people in our lives. Focus on that inner circle first. Our spouse, our children, our parents. Then we should work our way outward from there. I believe with just that one act of focus it will bring an amplified feeling of love, joy and success that often alludes us.

Dave W. Wadsworth   "Living" in the Ditch

"*Living*" in the *Ditch*
1-Ditch, 2-Boys & 3,000-Adventures

Snakes Alive -- Reflection and Action

WOW, that was a scary chapter.

Action 1.   **Write** briefly about a childhood memory that involved a snake and your interaction with it.

Action 2. **Plan and do** something this week that will bring back that same sense of excitement and adventure you shared in Action 1. **Write about it here & now:**

Action 3. **Plan** an activity you can **do each week** to take you back to that amazing child-like carefree world. Be sure it is not Illegal, Immoral or Fattening. (Insert Smile)

4. Turtle Love

Lunge, Snap, Hiss, Hiss, Recoil
........long Death Stare!

Lunge, Snap, Hiss, Hiss, Recoil...
.......long Death Stare!

This guy was <u>HUGE</u>, <u>DOUBLE UGLY</u> and <u>MAD</u>!!

MAD, yes he obviously was. Mad at who or what we weren't sure. Maybe he just got up on the wrong side of the ditch this morning. Maybe he didn't like two curious boys circling around and getting in his face. Maybe he was just one of those 8 or 9 really grouchy, miserable creatures on the planet.

Rabbit Trail for Jim Rohn:
(pronounced like Zone with an R)

Jim has passed on but his legacy looms large in the world of business, self-help and living the good life. Jim's teachings and impact are worldwide and historic. Much like his dear friend and another of my all-time favorite people, Zig Ziglar.

Jim Rohn was a personal mentor to the rich and famous such as Tony Robbins. At the same time, his humility, humor and compassion continues to be a personal awakening to the masses. Jim said his mentor told him that most people are generally decent, fine people. He said that there are only 8 or 9 really nasty miserable people in the world. He jokingly added that they seem to move around a lot. (Insert Laugh here)

I think that is an important lesson for us to carry inside our hearts daily. People are generally decent and actually have the same positive goals and aspirations that we do. Freedom, family, love and the opportunity to pursue genuine happiness and fulfillment.

I have to put this large angry beast into the category of the 8 or 9 miserable. In my many years I have encountered dozens of this particular type of beast and their nasty, bite-first and ask questions later, disposition remains constant.

This particularly large, ugly and angry fellow had wandered into our back yard that day. This beast had Doug and I on full-out fear (nearly pants wetting) alert. Doug & I circled the beast as it continued its severe, blunt warning;

Lunge, Snap, Hiss, Hiss, Recoil then a long Death Stare.

This guy was honestly as fast as greased lightning with his lunge & snap. His head and neck struck fast and furious like an angry rattlesnake. "Wow Doug, what do we have here?", I asked nervously. "Well, Doug stammered, it's a huge, creepy & mad turtle". "I know it's a huge, creepy, angry turtle, Sherlock".

"What kind of huge, creepy, angry turtle is it?" I again requested. "I don't know, Doug said, but it is super-scary and not a happy camper".

Its' coloring was black or very dark brown. His body looked like an alligator that went through a huge kitchen blender and came out in the shape of a turtle. His skin and features looked tough, rugged, and leathery. He was, by all accounts, bumpy, ugly, and angry enough to eat nails.

He acted like he was mad at the world. As we waved a small stick near its face the lunge and snap action quickly and savagely splintered it. Large and small stick pieces went flying in several directions. This was pretty awesome, we thought. But again we had that question in our minds; What is this beastly thing? As Doug and I circled and got too close again, the powerful head and razor sharp jaws instantly thrust to bite off any toes that got too close.

----Lunge, Snap, Hiss, Hiss, Recoil......Death Stare.

Rabbit Trail for Death Stare clarity:

You remember the Death Stare as a child, don't you? The kind that your mom would give you when you acted up in a public place. (As a married, sometimes clueless guy, your wife occasionally flashes it your way; wink, wink.)   Back to Mom. You remember those times she couldn't wail on your butt, like you deserved, right then?

She is helplessly stuck between abandoning a full cart of groceries, in the checkout lane AND summoning super strength to make it to the car before exploding on your fanny.

All she could do was give you the "Death Stare" that seemed to burn a hole right through you. You understood that message to mean a good spanking was coming at home, if we made it that far with our butts intact.

Well, that was a soft glowing candle stare compared to the laser mega death stare this angry beast was sending our way. This was one bad, scary dude.

After a few more minutes of circling we (I) had a plan. I said "Doug, you stay here and keep this beast busy while I run and get dad to save the day". "Ok", Doug nervously replied. Then I bolted before Doug could figure out that he would be barefoot and all alone with the beast. Sacrifice little brother to the creature while I run for help. The plan sounded good to me.   Instantly I found myself sprinting for the house where I knew dad was doing his yard work.

Without a second wasted, an excited and out of breath little boy had rushed to where dad was working.

"Dad, come quick, we need you", I exclaimed excitedly. "It's this monster turtle in our back yard". "Hurry dad, come quick we need you". "It's this monster turtle" I keep saying. For some reason dad didn't seem too interested in joining our monster turtle adventure. He was busy and quite calmly answered saying "oh, it's probably just a Snapping Turtle". I kept begging for dad to come see it and share the adventure. I sensed his disinterest so when I ask him again and he repeated the line "oh, it's probably just a Snapping Turtle" I had to think of another convincing angle.   I was pretty sure he was right about it being a Snapping Turtle but I wanted him to come with me so badly that I exclaimed "oh, no it's not a Snapping Turtle" (Insert little white lie here). Again I said "oh, no dad it's not a Snapping Turtle so you have to come see.

Rabbit Trail for Crazy Legs:

Do you remember those times, as a child, when you were so excited to go somewhere that your legs took over and you just started hopping and skipping and running along uncontrollably? Your body was so amped up you couldn't keep from skipping and bouncing with excitement. When I convinced dad to come check out this huge attack turtle my body just went jumping jack crazy.

As an adult, this is where we have squashed that excitement somewhere deep down inside. We need to fight to get back to that child-like excitement we have buried. When I see adults experiencing this I'm truly happy for them. At the same time, I find myself a bit jealous, disappointed and angry that I haven't fought to return there myself.

Pete Carroll, head coach of the NFL Seattle Seahawks football team, is a great example of this. Although I don't know Pete personally, my heart literally sings when I watch the multiple expressions of fun and enjoyment he displays while coaching his team. Years ago, while watching Pete coach the USC Trojans, I remember that same child-like enthusiasm bursting through as he interacted with his players and coaches on the sideline. I confidently tell myself that Pete is a man who has found his "Crazy Legs" as an adult. Congratulations to coach and may we all seek to unearth those buried hopping, skipping and bouncing emotions of the past.

Back to the Big, Ugly, Angry Beast:

Reluctantly dad put his tools down and began to follow me to the back yard.
 As we got closer I was sure hoping Doug hadn't let the beast escape. More importantly, I thought to myself, gee whiz, I hope my little brother hadn't gotten eaten by this huge turtle. Rounding the corner of our house I caught a glimpse of Doug still out back near where I had left him alone with the beast. Whew! He wasn't eaten and I could now see that the huge turtle was still there. Bouncing and skipping along I reached Doug and the turtle well before dad got there. It seemed like that thing had grown since I left and I sure was glad that dad would soon join us to save the day.

When dad walked close I could see Doug relax a bit. It really made Doug nervous being left alone with this massive turtle. Dad soon joined us near the turtle and said "yep, like I said, it's just an old Snapping Turtle". Doug and I looked at each other as if to say "Our dad sure is smart, he knows everything about everything ". Ok, I reluctantly admitted, "Dad you were right".   But Dad this is a really big and scary monster Snapping Turtle. At that, dad laughed and began telling us about his many experiences with snappers like this one.

Dad always amazed us with his endless knowledge of so many things. He sensed our fears and so he began leading us along with an old wives-tale about huge snappers. Dad was very convincing and he began reeling us in. It wasn't long until this whopper-of-a-tale we willingly swallowed hook, line, and sinker. (A fishing expression that means we were totally believing his story).

Dad played around with the snapper, teasing it with a large stick as he continued the tale. The lightning quick lunge and snap reflexes were scary to witness. Dad began talking about how fierce these ancient fighting snappers were. He warned how it's razor sharp jaws had been known to take off fingers and toes all the way to the knuckle. Not even a bloody stub left over. His eyes glistened and focused intently on us. Now hanging on each word, we were both excited and scared.

When dad said "bloody stub" the two barefoot little boys, only inches away, instantly looked down as if to count all 10 of our toes again. After all our toes were found still attached we were very thankful we hadn't gotten within striking distance. Running barefoot near this toe eating monster was not a good idea.

Dad really had us going as he continued on about his years of knowledge and experience with many species of turtles including these vicious snappers. He then starred at us with a very serious look and said firmly, "boys, you have to stay away from these big Snapping Turtles". We both looked intently into his eyes mesmerized by the seriousness of the message. We were eagerly anticipating the gem of turtle wisdom he was about to impart. We both knew he meant business and we were drinking it in. Dad could see he had our full attention and then he unloaded the tales' shocking punch line.

Dad confidently stated "now boys, these snappers are extremely dangerous. "They are so mean and so dangerous that if you get too close and they bite you"......Dad paused to draw us in tight; "Well", he continued "if they bite you (slight pause) they won't let go of you until it thunders. The seriousness never left his face and our eyes were fixed on his with near disbelief.

We stood frozen, in our tracks, while our young minds tried to process just how long that would be. They wouldn't let go until it thunders, we questioned? Our minds then spoke to us saying, "that would mean it would have to storm and then flashes of lightning and finally the thunder would sound off".

Wow, at that moment Doug and I both looked up into the clear blue summer sky to scan for any approaching storm clouds. We just couldn't wrap our head around the concept that this monster turtle would hang on to our little hand or foot until it would thunder. That could mean hours, or days or, oh-my-gosh, a week? We would have to go to school with this beast dragging along like a prisoner's ball and chain. Unbelievable.

Again, we had always trusted dad's wise words. For some reason the excitement of this event wouldn't allow our minds to catch hold of his old wives-tale story. This time I can honestly confess that the, thunder clapping before a snapper would release its' bite thing, rattled around in my brain for a long, long time. It may have been weeks or months before it was ever fully resolved.

We can sure laugh about it now. At the time, it was just another big story that dad calmly and masterfully weaved together. After the weaving he would always manage to slowly suck us in. Dad was awesome the way he led us on with such great stories. What a cool dad. We sure were two lucky boys. Dad taught us all about the awesomeness of nature and we kept all 10 of our toes.

The title of this chapter is "Turtle Love" and that's what 99% of our turtle encounters were. In spite of the giant snapper adventure we mostly had fun and happy turtle times in the ditch. Even future Snapping Turtle events were positive as we normally caught very small and much less threatening ones.

The small snappers still seemed to carry that nasty angry attitude but we could easily catch and safely play with them. They would bite on a stick and then we could carry them around as they clung to the stick. This was really entertaining to carry a turtle which had just bit down on a stick. And, of course, like dad said, we carried them dangling by their clinched jaws until it finally thundered. Ha, Ha, just kidding. I got you there.

Truthfully we would hold them by the tail or far back on their shell which usually worked out ok. Well, hang on just a second, I need to count my toes again to verify that: 6,7,8,9,10. Ok, all good here. Ha-ha.

Like the crawdads, the turtles were animals we liked to catch and play with. After about a half hour of fun and game playing we would let them loose to crawl back into the ditch safe and sound.

Box turtles were very colorful with yellow and dark brown color all over. They were built funny and were able to completely close up in their shells for protection against predators and very curious little boys.

I had a stubborn streak and I really liked playing with the turtles. I learned that if I waited long enough they would "come out of their shells". They would eventually realize we weren't going to hurt them and you could tell they relaxed and became more playful.

I would say that we enjoyed dozens of turtles during our childhood summers. I remember that the turtles came in many splendid colors, shapes and sizes. They were all pretty shy when they saw the two barefoot boys coming close.

Green turtles were both regular finds and fun play partners. These little fellas were dark green with some areas of lighter green. They had black colors mixed in with lots of yellow on their bellies. Then we had green turtles that were almost exactly the same green colors but they had a very cool red patch on their neck and head area.   We called these the "Red Eared Turtles".

Several summers in a row we got to catch and play with a little Green Turtle that had been injured on one leg. It looked like a mean old snapper had bit half or more of its' toes off the right front leg. The wound had healed and didn't' seem to bother his swimming too much. We did notice he had a little sideways swimming action. It was kind of like a little boy running with the limp from a sprained ankle. It worked but it wasn't the best situation. It was so cool that this little fellow was around many summers since we all enjoyed living in the ditch.

Painted Turtles were really beautiful to see. They had a fabulous mixture of colors including the various greens and lots of yellow. These guys also had many areas of red coloring that made them so unique and lovely. The Painted Turtles had the same body types and personalities of the Green Turtles. These painted turtles loved the water and rarely did we see them out of the water. They loved to set out in the sun on half sunken logs and large branches. As we waded up and downstream, in the ditch, we would come around a corner and startle these little log sunning guys. They would quickly scramble into the water and swim away to hide in the aquatic weeds. I was fascinated to see how fast they swam and how they were constantly on alert with a specific escape plan.

Box Turtles were both fun and beautiful playmates for two little boys. Doug and I would normally find the Box Turtles roaming our yard or eating strawberries in our garden. Dad spent long hours tending our huge garden and produced amazing amounts of many vegetables. He was always happy when we moved the invading Box Turtles out from munching his fresh produce. The Box Turtles were also very plentiful in the small woods just north of Grandma and Grandpa Orender's house.

Box Turtles were the shyest of all the many turtles we encountered. On a shyness scale they were easily a 10 (super scared) while the snappers were a solid #1 (not at all shy). Actually the snappers were very aggressive and would often charge at you with the slightest provocation. If you remember the "Bloody Stubs" we talked about then you quickly realize a charging Snapping Turtle can be reason for barefoot boys to be concerned.

Box Turtles were quick to withdraw completely back into their shells. Most of the turtles couldn't completely close their shells. These guys were slick and snug like one of mom's plastic Tupper Ware containers. They had a brown and yellow rounded shell like a warped softball with a flat bottom. The brown and yellow colors made a really cool pattern like one of those patch-work quilts my grandma Floy Wadsworth used to make.

The top of the shell was much darker than the bright yellow and light brown belly of the shell. When frightened, the Box Turtle would pull it's legs all the way inside and seal up the shell. At the same time, it's head would pull back in and the lower shell front would close up tight like a trap door. When closed up it was slanted like a smooth car loading ramp.   This was an amazing sight to behold. These Box Turtles were very shy and we would wait a long time for them to finally open the hatches and, …..well,…….. come out of their shells. This took a lot of patience for two little boys to set still long enough to watch this all unfold. Many times we just gave up and went on to other adventures.

I remember a few times waiting long enough for these Box Turtles to come out and start walking again. On rare occasions one would get brave enough to stay out of its' shell and "air walk" while we held it. I guess after so long they realized that the two barefoot boys were just curious and meant them no harm. I remember their chubby little legs would be covered with tiny scales like those on a dragon. These scales looked like they were glued on and often were a beautiful yellow, brown and even bright orange color.

Oh, before I forget. These Box Turtles would suck back in their shells so tight we couldn't get them out until they wanted to come out. I even remember using our fingers, fingernails and small sticks to try to get them open but never succeeded. It was as hopeless as two kids with a coconut shell. Not gonna happen.

Before our turtle adventures swim away I must tell of our encounter with the strangest turtle of all. One late sunny afternoon I was standing high on the ditch bank in front of our house. As I looked down at the ditch I spotted this strange looking creature. His neck was stretched way out in front as he swam rapidly upstream. He swam completely under water and although he was certainly out of place he acted like he was on a mission to somewhere important. He was a solid dark tan or light brown color. He was also round like a Frisbee and about the size of a large supper plate.

Doug was around behind our house getting fishing supplies so I had to yell really loud to get his attention. He knew by my excited shouts that something serious was going on with me in the ditch. Doug dropped his gear and ran as fast as he could around our house to join me.

We quickly rushed down the bank to get a closer look at this odd turtle. Neither of us had ever seen such a creature in our ditch. Doug's eyes got really big as his mind tried to take it all in. He was trying to figure out just exactly what this new beast was. Doug said "look at his nose, it's got a funny point on the end like a blunt target arrow".

We both grabbed a stick and planned how we would subdue this strange creature. Any critter that dared to swim in our ditch was subject to capture and close inspection before allowed to go on its' merry way. We could tell it wasn't a mean and vicious Snapping Turtle but since this was our first encounter we were very cautious in our approach.

I soon realized our two sticks couldn't do the trick so I sent Doug scrambling after one of our large wire mesh open topped fishing traps. We then cornered and sized up our creepy quarry. With our two sticks we were soon able to coax him into the wire trap and get him up on the bank for closer examination. At first he struggled and tried to dig into the green moss and muddy bank to get away. Very soon he would know that the two barefoot boys were beast masters and kings of this ditch. In just a few minutes this funny looking turtle was subdued and carried safely about halfway up the ditch bank.

The strange round turtle was pretty mild mannered but we didn't want to take any chances by getting our bare fingers or toes near his mouth. Doug and I were both amazed at the weird features of this new turtle we had captured. We gently poked and pushed around on the turtles' body to get a good look at all his weirdness.

We rolled him over and spun him around several times to figure out this mysterious fellow. We both quickly agreed that this was the only turtle we had ever seen with a shell not hard like a rock. This guys' shell was soft and pliable like a brown piece of thick rubber. I exclaimed to Doug that "this guy was round and leathery and looked just like our buddy Jeffs' catcher's mitt". The color and texture was the same only this guy had legs and a head. We had no idea why his shell would be like that and it reminded us of the "soft shelled" crawdads we would rarely find in the ditch. Maybe he had a birth defect or something. Truly weird.

We probably spent a total of 30 minutes checking this guy out. With our curiosity satisfied we gently returned him unharmed into the ditch so he could continue his upstream swimming quest.

That evening dad patiently listened to our long tale of this latest turtle adventure. Can you believe it? When we finished the story dad was able to explain to us that it was called a Soft Shelled Turtle. Again we were amazed at how smart our dad was. I sure loved and admired my dad. And so it was with all the really cool turtle stories and two barefoot boys "living" in the ditch.

"*Living*" in the *Ditch*
1-Ditch, 2-Boys & 3,000-Adventures

Turtle Love -- Reflection and Action

WOW, that Snapping Turtle was sure scary.

Action 1.   **Write** briefly about a childhood memory that involved a turtle and your interaction with it.

Action 2. **Plan and do** something this week that will bring back that same sense of joy and adventure you shared in Action 1. Write your plan here:

Action 3. Plan an activity you can **<u>do each week</u>** to take you back to that amazing child-like carefree world. Be sure it is not Illegal, Immoral or Fattening. (Insert Smile)

5. **Minnows & Fish**

"Dave, grab the net". "Hurry, grab the net". "It's a Gar", Doug shouted. When I heard the word gar I started flying across the yard to retrieve the closest fishing net I could find. "Keep an eye on him", I yelled back at Doug. A Gar was a very strange and a fairly rare sight, in the ditch.

The Gar and Snapping Turtle were kindred spirits in my book. Both were prehistoric in appearance and they shared that angry nasty disposition. They would prefer to bite you first and ask questions later. Actually, I think they would just bite you and leave you for dead without asking questions. The Snapping Turtle was a toothless beast with lightning fast attacks and razor sharp jaws. The Gar swam in lightning fast bursts of speed and had a mouth full of razor sharp teeth.

The Gar was long, slender and ugly as a mud fence. The ones patrolling our ditch were typically 10 to 15 inches long and round like a jumbo hotdog sold at the baseball park. Yep, a torpedo with teeth. Like the Snapping Turtle, they were at the top of the fish food-chain. If they invited you to dinner it wasn't a friendly social invitation. It was your "last supper". To be real honest here, they tried to eat me several times. Of course it was a finger or chunk of skin at a time. Boy, they sure liked to bite. Fearless, feisty and fast.

Catching a Gar required cat like reflexes and a precisely executed plan of attack. All the ditch creatures had their fast get-away techniques. That meant each one required a different hunting approach. The gars would allude capture more than any fish and nearly as often as the large snakes. Once a large snake got in the tall weeds, along the far ditch bank, it was nearly impossible to find and catch. I think our fear of getting snake bit made us much more cautious when corralling a large snake. The Gar was limited to swimming in the water but they displayed jet-like speed. They could really turn on the after burners when they sensed danger.

Doug and I stood high on the ditch bank discussing our capture plan for this mean old Gar. We kept a keen eye on the wily old fish since it's speedy nature gave us very little room for error. The Gar would float in the water as still as a rock. It looked like it wore army camo because of the blotchy color mix of light green, dark green, brown and black. These guys were stealthy, like a feral cat, and always on the lookout for unsuspecting fish.

Doug and I knew from past experience that when we got near a gar it would zoom, dash and dart its' way to safety. I instructed Doug to stay high on the bank as he made his way about 40 feet upstream and far ahead of the Gar. I would take the net and slowly work my way into the water about 10 feet downstream of the Gar. I always kept constant eye contact with this worthy opponent.

On my signal, Doug slowly made his way toward me always keeping the Gar between us. Doug was the aggressor and when he approached I would relay exactly where the Gar was and how close he was at all times. Keeping the Gar in an area where the ditch was shallow also gave us a better chance of success. While Doug steadily moved in I would remain completely still just a few feet downstream.

Doug would pin the unsuspecting Gar near one bank. Then as it would turn it darted right into my net at the last second.   Like a speeding bullet the Gar would hit my net and be stunned for about a second. At the very instant it hit my net I had to lift the net out of the water and flip the Gar up onto the bank. That booger was so fast and would flip flop so high he was really hard to contain.

I always heard people say that curiosity killed the cat. I can honestly say curiosity also got Doug and Dave Gar-bit on many occasions. We were fascinated by its' strange, ugly looks & feisty nature.   The gar was always a serious challenge to capture.   After we played

Dave W. Wadsworth   "Living" in the Ditch

around and examined the Gar it was time to chuck it back into the ditch. We weren't as gentle with these feisty fellas.

Minnows of all kinds were abundant up and down the ditch. They came in so many cool shapes, colors and sizes. We had our own names for each type and loved the challenge of catching each one. Toppers and Chubbys were the most common while Shiners and Baby Cat sightings were usually pretty rare.

Toppers were kind of like the majestic male lion of the minnows. They would swim alone or in small groups of two or three. We figured these grew up to be bass since they had a lot of similar features. Toppers were long and skinny with a grey and green body coloring. Two unique features included a single large white dot on top of their head and a black line that ran down their side.

Fish Quiz:
Can you guess where we would always find these minnows swimming? That's correct. Along the

114

Dave W. Wadsworth   "Living" in the Ditch

"TOP" of the water. Toppers were content to swim near the bank but not too interested in moving up or down stream. Because they stayed very still, in the water, it was sometimes hard to locate them in and around the moss. If we waded close to the Toppers they could really dart around and swim in rapid short bursts of speed.

Chubbys were shorter than the Toppers and they would swim much slower as well. Chubbys were bloated looking and resembled a mix between a fish and a large tadpole. I'll tell you all about tadpoles when we get to the chapter on frogs. I think the Chubbys grew up to be Bluegills and Sunfish but I could be wrong. I didn't have the time or patience to set along the ditch and watch the growing process for weeks at a time. It was just a hunch.

Do you remember when we talked about the ditch damming adventures in chapter 1? Good, well, as the ditch would wind its' way along our property the water would cut and fill shallow and deeper pockets. This was caused by currents and obstacles like sticks and rocks. These pockets would get as much as 20 inches deep and create havens for a whole host of awesome critters. The big granddaddy crawdads loved them and also the lightning fast minnows we called Shiners.

Shiners were always found in large groups of twenty or more and they stayed mostly in these deep pools. Shiners were long and slender like Toppers but fast and fidgety. They were in a constant motion zipping around each other playfully like tiny little Dolphins.

They looked like dancing fish with shiny silver bellies that they took turns flipping over. Amazingly, as they swam down deep they were somewhat hard to keep track of. All the sudden, when they flipped sideways, the afternoon sun would reflect sharply and it looked like a constant flashing of beautiful lights. It reminded me of the steady flash from photographers along the red carpet on Oscar night in Hollywood. Wow, that was a beautiful sight to behold.

Grounders were funny minnows that also liked to swim in groups and usually numbered about a dozen. These guys had the exact same coloring as the majestic Topper minnows but didn't have the distinguishing white dot on their head. Grounders used the same fidgety swimming pattern as Shiners but didn't hang out in the deep pools. These guys were often on the move headed up or downstream as if they were on a mission. Once in a while they would stay in a fairly shallow pool and dance for the afternoon and then be gone by morning.

I remember the first time I saw a swimming ball of black Baby Cats. It was so cool. I was by myself when I spotted what looked like a black tennis ball of wiggling strange creatures swimming slowly along our side of the ditch.   I had to get a much closer look and find out just what this wiggly mass was all about. I quickly slipped off my shoes and stepped into the water.   When I bent down for a closer look I couldn't believe my eyes. Catfish. Little, itty bitty teeny tiny cute baby Catfish.

They were swimming and frolicking along in one big ball. It looked like 25 or 30 of the cute little rascals. Being a Ditch Master I just had to get a jar and catch a couple to make my thorough examination. They moved pretty slow so with a large mouth jar I scooped in and easily captured three of the wigglers. They were black as coal and perfectly shaped miniature catfish only about 1-inch long.

OUCH!! The sharp pricking pain let me know that these little boogers were fully equipped with sharp spines on each side and top just like full grown Catfish. The ditch was chocked full of harmful, prickly, pinching, biting, sticking, scratching and cutting creatures, plants and objects. Doug and I experienced the pain of them all with second and third helpings on most.

We painfully found out that the large Catfish liked to bite. They would give you a swift and painful bite with a lot of force and tiny little teeth.   We also found out that those side and top spines were like monster sized needles. Wow, those drew blood and hurt like the dickens.   These Catfish had lots and lots of teeth but lucky for us, they were very small teeth. Even with the small teeth they could sure shock you when they snapped their mouth shut on your little fingers. Oh well, I guess that's the price you pay for living in the ditch.

Yes, indeed, these two little barefoot boys were sure lucky that Toppers, Grounders, Shiners, Cubby's, Baby Cats, Gars, Bass, Bluegill, Sunfish and Chanel Catfish were all abundant and flourished in our ditch.

"*Living*" in the *Ditch*
1-Ditch, 2-Boys & 3,000-Adventures

Minnows & Fish -- Reflection and Action

WOW, all those fun fish stories.

Action 1. <u>Write</u> briefly about a childhood memory that involved minnows and fish and your interaction with them.

Action 2. <u>Plan and do</u> something this week that will bring back that same sense of joy and adventure you shared in Action 1. <u>Write</u> out your plan here, in this book!

Action 3. <u>**Plan**</u> an activity you can <u>**do each week**</u> to take you back to that amazing child-like carefree world. Be sure it is not Illegal, Immoral or Fattening. (Insert Smile)

6. Little Blood Suckers

"Mom, help me", I yelled. Get the matches and burn this thing off. These little guys were nasty little blood suckers. Parasites of the first degree. Creepy and leathery and always attached to our feet and legs after a day of wading in the ditch. They were a dark brown leathery beast usually about the size of a quarter or half dollar. They weren't very thick but they could stretch and change shape in amazing ways. I remember watching one swim through the water and it stretched itself out several inches long and became skinny like a thick strand of moms knitting yarn.

When they attached to our skin they would usually be in a flattened pear or tear drop shape.

Leeches were just one of our blood sucking enemies from the ditch. Doug and I would constantly have to get mom to rescue us from their clutches. Their back was leathery and rough but the underneath side was as smooth as silk. They would latch onto our skin at both ends of their strange little bodies.

I remember my blood flowing from each end when mom would burn them off of us. She would run and get the big box of kitchen matches and we would meet her on the front porch. We would stick our leg up close and she would strike a match and touch the burning tip against the clinging little blood sucker. Some of the big ones didn't want to let go right away but a second match would be convincing enough.

These brown leeches were like a chunk of tough rubber. Once mom got them to come off our leg or foot we would grab a rock and smash them on our concrete sidewalk. Since they always made me bleed I did get some enjoyment out of squashing them with the rock. They were weird little rubbery goobers without eyes or arms or legs of any kind. They didn't seem to hurt while they were attached and sucking away. I will have to admit that their creepy factor was pretty high up the scale.

Ticks, ticks and more ticks. Little creepy suckers. Every day we lived in the ditch we always brought in a tick or 5! These guys were much smaller than the leeches but I hated them more. They were creepy crawly like a spider and I always got the heebie geebies from spiders. You will have to wait for the chapter on ditch spider adventures to hear some really good stuff on them.

The ticks were always in the grass or weeds near the ditch. These goobers would crawl out to the end of a branch or leaf and wait with their claws out just waiting for us to walk by. They would use their front meat hook type legs to snag on when we walked close and brushed against where they stood ready. Once the creepers got on you they just started crawling around looking for a good place to dig in and start sucking your blood.   Lots of time they would crawl to the waist band of our shorts or, well, in our private parts. We found ticks in our hair a lot and so mom would have to give us a thorough tick check every time we came in from playing, in the ditch.

Harry and Bacon were our two pet dogs when we were kids. Harry was a sweet natured and passive short haired Beagle. Bacon, well, he was just the opposite. Bacon was black as coal except for the one white spot on his throat. When our neighbors gave Bacon to us he was just a chubby little fur-ball puppy. He was so excited to play with us boys that he peed all over our living room floor just 10 minutes after arriving. Dad was mad and nearly made the neighbors take him back. He was an incredible bundle of energy and didn't have a speed except for full blast. Bacon was a cocker spaniel and border collie mix with frizzy hair going everywhere.

Ticks absolutely love dogs and the long haired dogs were especially easy targets. Harry and Bacon were always having to be checked and all the ticks removed. Bacon was so wooly it was a major battle holding him still and digging down to find all the ticks.

After eating a huge meal, like Thanksgiving, mom and dad used to say they were "stuffed like a tick". While taking care of our two dogs I soon realized what that expression meant. I remember finding ticks on Bacon that we had missed and they were swollen like little marbles. They were big and dark blue and would absolutely explode with blood when squeezed too hard. Yuk. Nasty. Ok, too much information there.

Dog Ticks are what mom and dad called the ones that latched onto us. They were a medium brown color. The color was like an older penny that has lost its' shine. I was always amazed how they could crawl on you and cling like Velcro.

They must have tiny little Spiderman barbs because you can't hardly shake them off. The ticks were all about the same size and color but some would have a distinct white spot on their back just like the Topper minnows.

When we got a tick that had dug deep, into our skin, mom would bring out the big box of kitchen matches again. Just like the leaches I think she enjoyed giving them the hot shot treatment. With ticks, mom would blow out the match right after lighting it and then touch the still hot match to the tick.

She would do this several times and then I think the tick usually decided to back his head out and get moving. If he wouldn't budge or she was too aggressive and burned him to death, then out came the tweezers and sewing needle for minor surgery. Mom was always protecting her barefoot boys from these blood sucking little beasts.

"*Living*" in the *Ditch*
1-Ditch, 2-Boys & 3,000-Adventures

Little Blood Suckers -- Reflection and Action

WOW, that chapter brings back creepy memories that really "suck".

Action 1.   **Write** briefly about a childhood memory that included ticks, leaches or other blood suckers and your interaction with them.

Action 2. **Plan and do** something this week that will help you avoid bad or dangerous encounters with blood suckers. Write it out here:

Action 3. <u>**Plan**</u> an activity you can **<u>do each week</u>** to take you back to that amazing child-like carefree world. Be sure it is not Illegal, Immoral or Fattening. (Insert Smile)

7.   Cutting Our Feet Off

**"You boys are going to cut your feet off"!!
"You get your boots on and I mean it"!!
"For the love of Pete, I'm telling you, your gonna cut your feet off"!!**

Mom, bless her heart, she would yell at us until she ran out of voice or strength or both. She was right to be concerned but we were two rambunctious barefoot boys without the sense or fear like most rational adults. The constant threat of tetanus, lockjaw and all those other nasty things were real but not to Doug and I. Mom talked about Lock-Jaw several times. I wasn't sure about it but I would picture going around with a padlock attached to my face somehow. Even though Lock-Jaw sounded really weird I couldn't bring myself to get too shook up about it.

Oh, my gosh. The bottom just broke out of my glass jar and all my captured fish just fell back into the ditch and escaped. Bummer, I thought to myself. Oh no, what is that strange feeling on my ankle? Looking down my eyes got big and my mind jumped to panic mode. In a funny (strange thought) my mind said to me; "Wow Dave, that's a lot of blood running out of the side of your ankle".

Maybe, I should head for home and give up our ditch adventure for the day. I don't know what happened but we were catching fish upstream in the large pool near the road bridge. All the sudden the large glass mason jar just came apart. Most of the jar stayed in my hand but the whole bottom and part of one side just cut loose.

We would carry the jars from the top with our thumb inside and our fingers clinging to the outside.

Sometimes when we needed a second hand we would briefly pin the jar between our hip and the inside of our forearm. By now there was enough blood flowing that I decided to walk up the bank and hike across the neighbors' yard since it was the quickest path to home.

Mom was always ready with the first aid kit. First aid always included pouring on the hydrogen peroxide. This clear liquid instantly foamed up really big. It was mom's standard first aid move and it acted as a wound cleaner before bandages could be applied. This time it was a very clean horizontal cut across the top of my ankle. The blood clotted pretty fast and she put on some nice bandage wrap so I was as good as new.

This cut was big and nasty enough to keep me out of the ditch for a few days though. When mom or Grandma Orender would mention "cutting our feet off" I could picture us walking around the yard on two bloody stub legs with no ankles or feet. Isn't it funny the images we get in our young minds from the things adults say.

I remember mom always warning us about rough-housing with sticks. She warned that we could poke an eye out. I always thought that sounded funny. I would think; with a stick you would actually poke your eye in? Right? Oh well, we survived it with all eyes intact.

Rabbit Trail for Bloody Stubs:

Speaking of bloody stubs;

Have you ever seen a chicken running around with its' head cut off? Well, Doug and I have. It is a crazy sight to behold. And did you know that chicken blood all over the yard is really sticky when you walk through it barefoot? Yuk & DoubleYuk.

Our neighbors Mildred and Paris Bratton were butchering a whole bunch of chickens one day. Now, of course Doug and I had to go check this strange operation out. They had chickens dangling from the clothes line which was a strange and new sight for us.

They also had set up some tables with pans on them. The bonus item was a huge monster sized boiling kettle of water. The next thing I noticed laying at the end of the table was enough knives to start a gang war.

A clothes line and chickens were common sights around Plainville but never together. The real shocker for us was seeing chickens hanging upside down on a clothes line. That was pretty radical and noisy to boot. Hold on now, it gets weirder than that. When Doug & I walked up we looked over just in time to see Mrs. Bratton coming out the back door with the biggest butcher knife we had ever seen. We both backed away trying to figure out what was coming next. We were still stunned to see chickens clucking and dangling from a clothes line and now Mrs. Bratton with that big knife.

We didn't have to wait long before the massacre began. It was savage and brutal for two sweet little boys to watch. Mrs. Bratton wielded that butcher knife like she was a Roman Gladiator. She started right down the line; Chicken number one—She grabbed the head with one hand and with one big slashing slice, of the knife, off comes the head.

Wow, now that was something you didn't see every day. Oh, get this. Immediately following the chicken decapitation, the dangling headless chicken bodies would start jumping around like, well, uh, "A Chicken With Its' Head Cut Off" I guess. It was like those dudes were still alive and they were dancing and jiggling trying to get away. Of course the clucking stopped. (sorry, sick humor there)

One of the "headless chickens" bounced so much his feet slipped out of the brackets holding him to the clothes line. He fell to the ground and you know what happened next? You don't? He ran around the yard in circles like a (now you guessed it) …. "A chicken with his head cut off". Honest John. I saw it with my own eyes.

Enough with the "chicken" blood and guts. Back to the ditch and our own blood n guts.

Cutoff jean shorts and a t-shirt were the everyday attire for Doug and I. No rubber boots, sneakers or flip flops for protecting our feet.   Hey, the ditch bottom was only loaded with countless thorns, broken glass, discarded pieces of sharp rusty metal, pointed sticks and sharp edged rocks. It is truly amazing that we didn't cut our feet off.

Scrapes, cuts and bloodletting was a daily thing for two barefoot boys. Glass and broken brick bats were very common along with rusty metal cans and sharp sticks. I remember puncturing my feet with thorns that were longer than my fingers. There was a big old thorn tree along the south bank that occasionally dropped those huge monster sized thorns in the water.   Thorn trees grow single thorns with many points as well as these huge clusters of all sizes of needle sharp thorns.   This particular tree grew thorns that varied in length from one inch to over 6 inches.

Only a few times do I remember that we put on boots to wade in the ditch. I think they only lasted a few minutes before they overtopped with water and we chucked them on shore for safe keeping. We couldn't have boots full of water slowing us down. We were chasing an endless bounty of fish, snakes, crawdads, frogs, bugs and turtles. We had to be free to run and capture our escaping prey. We were the two barefoot, undisputed champion "Ditch Masters".

We have all the cuts, scrapes and scars to prove it.

The End.

I'm sorry we didn't get to the Frogs, Spiders, Fence #5 and other great adventures. I will have to leave that for another day. Thanks for reading along and I truly challenge you to search to bring back your "Crazy Legs" of joy, excitement and passion of your childhood.

Dave W. Wadsworth   "Living" in the Ditch

"*Living*" in the *Ditch*
1-Ditch, **2**-Boys & **3,000**-Adventures

"BONUS TIME"

"PALS" FORMULA

My Dad modeled a tremendously positive attitude for his family & friends alike. I was blessed to inherit his "look-for-the-good" attitude. In fact, my next book is entitled "Attitude before Underwear". In that book I will be detailing the life-changing "Attitude" formula that I have developed.

In January of 2016 I met my dear friend and professional speaking coach Kent Julian. He is a first rate person, family man, and speaker. The PALS formula came to me through my idea brainstorming at one of his training sessions that summer. I developed this simple formula and over dinner that evening I shared it with Kent and his wife. He shared my enthusiasm and encouraged me to develop this idea for my future speaking and training engagements.

I call my formula **PALS**.

<u>PALS</u> is actually my acronym for **P + A = LS.**

My speaking, coaching & training engagements involve implementing this formula into your Business, Organization or Family. Attitude is a critical success component every person should lock into their own minds.

Since we *all* have **P**roblems, and *all* truly desire **L**ife **S**uccess, then that only leaves the critical bridge between those two; It is, simply put, our **A**ttitude.

P + A = LS formula and acronym is:

Problems + **A**ttitude = **L**ife **S**uccess.

No matter what anyone says to you.
No matter what anyone does to you.
No matter the circumstances that surround you.

Our Attitude is the one thing that we have 100% control of. It is Our choice how we respond to life & people. Not just a quick knee-jerk reaction. Reactions tend to be hurtful, damaging and actions we will soon live to regret. No matter how good or bad it seems, we ALWAYS have a choice of Attitude.

The critical bridge to LIFE SUCCESS is your ATTITUDE, pure and simple.

I strongly urge you to get and read the book titled "Man's Search for Meaning" by Viktor E. Frankl. In this book Viktor writes of personal experiences like none we could imagine in America today. Through all his physical, mental, and emotional torture he triumphs over death time and time again.

Although Viktor miraculously survived, he suffered the deaths of many friends, his young wife, his mom, his dad and his brother. The loss of his home. The loss of his early medical practice. The loss of all his possessions including his highly valued scientific writings. All of this on top of his subsequent imprisonment involving constant torture, hard labor and starvation.

One huge lesson that I learned from him was in his statement that "man's last freedom is his freedom to choose his ATTITUDE in any given situation of life". The choice of deciding "one's own way" at any point in life.

Every day, every hour and every minute we live is completely filled with the one thing called "CHOICES". We make hundreds and even thousands of choices each day. These choices come in all shapes, sizes and colors. Some are life changing but many are simple and mundane. To again quote the fabulous author, Andy Andrews, "we make choices and then over time those choices...make us".

That is the Dave Wadsworth paraphrase but it is so very true. For example: I did not walk into McDonald's one day and eat their daily "meal deal" and gain 110 extra pounds. They actually made it easy for me by installing a drive-thru window so I could stay in my air conditioned car. That made the cumulative weight gain much more rapid since I didn't burn any calories by getting out of my car and actually walking into the restaurant.

My ridiculous weight gains have not been through force feedings of large quantities of unhealthy food and drinks. Every single time I have intentionally got in my car and drove to these restaurants. I then asked for the exact unhealthy food I wanted. Then I actually pulled out my hard earned money and paid them for it.

This series of daily unhealthy choices was fully under my control. It all began with choices. I must boldly say that all of those choices began with my Attitude. If we all look close enough we can see that everything that we have become, is and was, based on our Attitude.

Chuck Swindoll is another of my favorite people in life and I want to share his famous poem on attitude with you here.

"ATTITUDE"

By Charles Swindoll

**THE LONGER I LIVE,
THE MORE I REALIZE THE IMPACT OF ATTITUDE
ON LIFE.
ATTITUDE TO ME, IS MORE IMPORTANT THAN
THE PAST,
THAN EDUCATION, THAN MONEY,
THAN CIRCUMSTANCES, THAN FAILURES,
THAN SUCCESS, THAN WHAT OTHER PEOPLE
THINK, OR SAY, OR DO.**

**IT IS MORE IMPORTANT THAN APPEARANCE,
GIFTEDNESS, OR SKILL.
IT WILL MAKE OR BREAK AN ORGANIZATION,
A SCHOOL, A HOME.**

THE REMARKABLE THING IS, WE HAVE A CHOICE EVERYDAY
REGARDING THE ATTITUDE WE WILL EMBRACE FOR THAT DAY.

WE CANNOT CHANGE OUR PAST.
WE CANNOT CHANGE THE FACT THAT PEOPLE WILL
ACT IN A CERTAIN WAY.
WE CANNOT CHANGE THE INEVITABLE.
THE ONLY THING WE CAN DO
IS PLAY ON THE ONE STRING WE HAVE,
AND THAT IS OUR ATTITUDE......

I AM CONVINCED THAT LIFE IS 10% WHAT HAPPENS TO ME
AND 90% HOW I REACT TO IT.
AND SO IT IS WITH YOU...

About the Author

Dave W. Wadsworth is a:

Generous, *Genuine* and *Uniquely Diverse* individual. He is an **Author**, **Motivational Speaker** and a **Business** & **Personal Coach**.

Dave produces the --------
--- **"Attitude 1st Radio Show"** --- which broadcasts worldwide each week. **Sarah**, his daughter, shares the Co-host honors on the show.

Dave also operates his own successful **Tree & Wildlife Management Business** that is the envy of most men (and many women).

Dave is a man of sincere **Faith**, strong **Family** values and a fierce defender of **Freedom** for all people.

Scientific testing by the Gallup Organization ranks Dave as the **Most Positive Person** on the planet.

His extensive travel and experience includes **Key Leadership** positions with the **U.S. Government, Corporations** and **Non-Profit Organizations**.

Dave W. Wadsworth   "Living" in the Ditch